CAREERS IN
LOGISTICS
SUPPLY CHAIN MANAGEMENT (SCM)

Inventory, Distribution, Transportation

LOGISTICS IS A TERM USED IN BUSINESS to describe the process of getting goods, supplies, equipment, and people where they need to be, when they need to be there. It is a specialized field that involves warehousing, inventory control, distribution, and transportation.

Logistics is an often overlooked field that most people do not usually think of when considering a future career. However, it plays a huge role in our economy and our everyday lives. American businesses currently spend more than $1.5 trillion on logistics each year. That gives some indication of how important logistics is to business. It also has a major impact on nearly everyone's daily lives. Without logistics we would not have hospitals, schools, electronics, mail, phones, sporting events, or TV. There would not be any food in the refrigerator either – unless you grew it yourself in your backyard.

Logistics managers are in charge of coordinating an organization's supply chain. It is a complex job that requires numerous steps. Using specialized computer software, they determine what and how many items are needed, how they will be acquired, how many will be stored in inventory, how they will be distributed, and what method of transportation will be used for delivery. Throughout the process, it is the logistics manager's responsibility to make sure it all goes smoothly. That often means thinking outside the box and brainstorming with team members to solve problems that are costing time and money. The goal is always to find the fastest, cheapest, and safest way to get things from point A to point B.

Logistics managers fill vital roles in organizations of all types and sizes. They work in nearly every industry and many government agencies. Nonprofit organizations, especially those involved in disaster relief, also depend on them to distribute lifesaving supplies to hot spots around the globe. The military also relies heavily on good logistics. In fact, the armed forces are where many logistics managers obtain their skills.

The number of jobs for logistics managers is growing, while employers often have trouble attracting new candidates. On any given day, there are thousands of job openings. The problem is not lack of rewards – the average pay for an experienced logistics manager is $100,000, not counting bonuses and other perks. It is because most people do not know about the excellent opportunities that await qualified candidates. How can you make yourself qualified? The surest way is to study logistics in college. Most employers want to see a bachelor's degree, but even a two-year associate degree or technical certificate is enough to get started. Employers also want to see motivation. An enthusiastic candidate with drive and leadership skills will always capture the attention of employers.

Do you love big trucks, trains, ships, and planes? Are you a people person who enjoys the camaraderie of working closely within a team? Logistics managers are in demand and people from all kinds of backgrounds are welcome to start in basic roles and work their way up. If you can multitask, handle responsibilities, and deal with pressure, you could have a secure future working in a comfortable office, or traveling the world doing exciting and challenging work.

WHAT YOU CAN DO NOW

ALTHOUGH IT IS QUITE POSSIBLE TO GET an entry-level job in logistics with only a high school diploma, it would be smart to prepare for college. Even a single year of post-high school education can increase earnings by thousands of dollars more a year. You can get that from a certificate program at a technical school or in an apprenticeship, but if you want a six figure income, you will need a bachelor's degree at some point. Therefore, you should ask your guidance counselor to help you develop a curriculum that meets standard college entry requirements.

Additional courses that will be helpful with your career aspirations include any business subjects, geography, and classes that promote good communications skills. A foreign language would make you particularly valuable to employers since you are likely to be either traveling overseas or coordinating with manufacturers, distributors, and shippers in other countries. Computer skills are also important in the daily work of logistics professionals. Learn to work with the basics like Microsoft Word, Excel, and PowerPoint. Many companies also use computer management systems to keep track of inventory and transportation, so look for opportunities to learn those systems as well. Research educational programs in your area or online that offer logistics or logistics management programs.

Try to learn more about logistics from professionals who currently work in the job you would like to have. Your guidance counselor can help you set up a job shadow or you can simply call a logistics provider in your town and ask to come and talk to someone about what the work entails. You can also read professional association newsletters and trade publications to get familiar with the field.

HISTORY OF THE CAREER

LOGISTICS TODAY IS A COMPLEX PROCESS that can move large quantities of goods across the globe. Centuries ago, it began in a much simpler form as a way to provide the military with troops, weapons, and other supplies in distant wars. The term "logistics" can be traced back to ancient Roman and Greek empires when the military officers who were responsible for distribution of resources were called "logistikas." Rome developed a particularly good logistics system that enabled soldiers to move forward efficiently. More than just a good system of transportation, it also involved defending supply locations and attacking those of the enemy.

During the Middle Ages, supply systems became more elaborate as logistics evolved into a business concept. Roads were built to provide easy movement between warehouses, which were forts and castles that had been repurposed as storage depots. By the onset of the Industrial Revolution, logistics had progressed through the building of vast railways and large cargo ships. During World War I, the development of the internal-combustion engine brought about the widespread trucking industry.

Logistics revisited its military roots during World War II. The US and its allies outperformed the German military, providing troops and supplies at the right time and right place. New logistical techniques were developed to provide more efficient and economical services. The allied forces were also able to do serious damage to German supply locations, while Germany was unable to do the same in return. Back in the US, major progress was being made in communications and transportation. Ships were built at an epoch pace, both for the military and the merchant marine that could move more goods, faster than ever, in and out of the country.

When the war ended, logistics was refocused on the business realm. Business was booming and getting orders filled and products into the hands of customers were primary concerns. Distribution, storage and warehousing, production planning, and customer service all became integral parts of the logistics process. By the 1950s, logistics managers needed to know much more about inventory control, supply costs, transportation options, and optimal warehouse locations. Logistics education was still very limited in scope at the time, so there was little opportunity for managers to learn about new concepts and techniques outside of the workplace.

Finally, in 1960, Michigan State University unveiled the first college course (along with the first textbook) that covered all aspects of outbound logistics. Shortly after, in 1963, the first professional association was formed under the name National Council of Physical Distribution Management (NCPDM). Founding members included companies in both the US and Canada. The unwieldy name was changed to the Council of Logistics Management in 1985.

The 1980s saw major advancements in the logistics field. The term "supply chain management" (SCM) was coined in 1982. Three years later, the textile and apparel industry was subjected to the first full scale supply chain analysis. Whether there is any difference between supply chain management and logistics management, other than a name, is a matter of debate that still continues today. SCM advocates claim it is an evolutionary step based on bold new concepts. SCM and logistics managers use the same basic techniques and ideas to manage product flows and make it possible for companies to expand international operations and compete in a global environment.

Another milestone development of the 1980s was the third party logistics (3PL) concept. Outsourcing of all kinds was extremely popular in the 1980s, and logistics was no exception. A number of 3PL companies sprouted and grew, as companies sought to save time and money and avoid the inevitable headaches of logistics activities. Today, nearly 90 percent of Fortune 500 companies use 3PL services. Some of the biggest names in the business use dedicated logistics companies that offer a level of logistics management that most individual companies cannot handle. Companies are spending billions to enlist the services of 3PLs like FedEx, UPS, Nippon, DHL, and Ryder.

Logistics management fully evolved as a profession in the 21st century. The US Department of Labor issued a classification for logisticians (really logistics managers) in the year 2000. At that time, e-commerce was still in its infancy and most people did not yet recognize how much it would change the landscape of business in general and retailing in particular. E-commerce has become the driving force for a global economy. Logistics managers in such an environment tackle a full gamut of e-commerce issues, from changing sourcing locations to safeguarding inbound cargo.

The biggest challenge for today's logistics managers is the retailing revolution that is taking place in every corner of the world, largely thanks to Amazon. Once a modest online seller of books, Amazon has grown into a mammoth international retailer of nearly 500 million items sold throughout the world. The company has literally changed the face of retail by turning traditional supply chain systems upside down. Amazon outsources its inventory management while keeping distribution and transportation logistics in house. This is the opposite of most giant retailers, both online and offline. Amazon determined that outsourcing would slow down delivery time. Through a complex web of partnerships and company-owned fleets, it is able to get products to hundreds of millions of customers in two days, the same day, and even within one hour.

Amazon's ongoing goal of delivering products to customers in the quickest possible time has changed the way supply chain management works. Every other player in the retail industry across the globe is under intense pressure to be faster, bolder, and more flexible.

It is an open question what the next disruptive force in logistics will be, but the field is in need of creative and innovative professionals who can respond with new and innovative means of supply and delivery.

WHERE YOU WILL WORK

BECAUSE THE SUCCESS OF BUSINESSES is so dependent on professionally designed and executed logistics, you can find logistics managers in nearly every industry. Some work in the logistics department of a company or nonprofit organization, while others work for the government. There are also third party logistics providers and other firms that specialize in logistics work, such as freight shipping and global forwarding companies.

The largest employers of these professionals are in manufacturing, which accounts for one out of every four jobs in logistics management. The second largest employer is the federal government. Other major areas of employment are retail, insurance, hospitality, healthcare, and construction. The military also spends money on logistics because it is often necessary to move large amounts of supplies and personnel from region to region. While employment can be found just about anywhere, certain cities such as Los Angeles and Chicago are considered hotspots for logistics.

The work logistics managers do is not location specific and there is no standard work setting. The workplace is most often an office, a factory floor, or a distribution center, but there are numerous other settings. Some even work remotely. Travel is very common. Domestic travel usually involves going from an office to a manufacturing plant, or a mobile location like a delivery or pickup center. Managers also travel overseas to visit customers and review supply chains.

The vast majority of logistics managers work full time on fairly regular schedules. However, overtime hours are common in order to ensure that problems are corrected quickly and operations stay on schedule. It may also be necessary to work evenings and weekends during peak seasons or when a company is undergoing major changes to operations. About one out of four managers works more than 40 hours per week.

THE WORK YOU WILL DO

THE MOST BASIC DEFINITION OF LOGISTICS is the transportation and storage of goods from the point of origin to the point of consumption. Logistics managers direct the movement of supplies and materials, consumer products, and people to wherever they need to be. In the process, they oversee activities that include purchasing, transportation, inventory, and warehousing. A typical logistics management job would involve overseeing a distribution facility, making sure everything is running smoothly. The manager would be responsible for seeing that the correct quantity of the right items leave the facility at the scheduled time, and are shipped to the right destination in the most efficient and cost-effective way possible.

Logistics plays a key role in modern life. In fact, it is the vital element that makes even the most common things possible. For example, it is unlikely you grew the food in your kitchen yourself. Everything from fresh fruits and cheese, to milk and cereal, to meat and canned goods, was moved from farms and processing facilities in multiple countries to your local grocery store or to the warehouse of a home delivery service. Without logistics, we would all still be farmers producing our own food.

Food is a simple example. Consider something more complicated, like ordering a smartphone from Amazon. That phone started out as a handful of raw materials. First, the materials had to be shipped to plants where they were turned into metal, plastic, glass, and silicon. This could be in another state or, more likely, a different country. The refined materials were then transported to other factories in another country where they became many small components. The components moved on again to yet another factory somewhere in the world where they were used to make the phone. Then the phone had to be sent to a distribution center where it was added to an inventory management system. At this point, you went online and with a couple of clicks, ordered the phone. The phone was taken out of the system (and accounted for), a delivery service was selected along with an ETA (estimated time of arrival), and finally sent to you with a tracking number to make sure it arrived. Logistics professionals were needed for every step along the phone's journey, from quarries and oil wells, to your hand.

A version of the same routine makes it possible to have medical care, entertainment, sports, housing, clothing, and even old fashioned snail mail. Without skilled logistics professionals, we would still be living in the Dark Ages with no TV, fast food, cars, laptops, or movies.

How the Work is Done

Transportation

The job description of a logistics manager includes numerous responsibilities, but one of the most important is ensuring efficient movement of goods through a company's shipping system. In the transportation sector, managers negotiate rates with transportation providers, such as airlines, trucking companies, global shipping firms, and "last mile" delivery services. They audit bills to make sure there are no overcharges, review customs documents and bills of lading, and when delivery problems arise they investigate and resolve them. They also generate reports that are used to analyze shipment delivery times for different quantities and weight.

Inventory

Logistics managers are also in charge of inventory. They make sure inbound products are in good condition and are stored correctly. Any damage is immediately documented. They record all inventory changes and input the data into a computerized system that keeps track of items by serial number. They monitor the flow, in and out, to accurately manage stock levels.

Distribution

Both transportation and inventory overlap with distribution. Managers assigned to distribution have a demanding job. They are responsible for making sure all orders are fulfilled correctly. That basically means getting the right products to the right location on time and at a low cost. They often liaise with suppliers of raw materials and manufacturers and may be tasked with sourcing new suppliers and negotiating prices to meet budgetary targets. They also deal with the other side of the equation, retailers and consumers, to ensure that expectations are met.

Throughout these processes, logistics managers are always on the alert for bottlenecks and other obstacles that need to be cleared up.

Logistics managers are usually in charge of teams or sectors within a larger logistics operation. The operation could be a big business, a third party logistics service firm, or military supply chain. They typically have supervisory duties, and are in charge of hiring, training, and firing employees. Depending on how large the organization is, they may request team leaders involved in warehouse, distribution, or shipping operations to provide detailed reports daily.

The primary tool of logistics management is software that is specially designed to manage logistical functions, such as planning and tracking the movement of people or goods, or managing inventory. Managers also use computers to process documentation, keep customer service logs, produce reports showing logistics performance, and maintain safety records. Much of this administrative work is done by the manager's support and administrative staff.

Starting Out

People starting out in logistics often work in customer service management or manage product inventory for a business, procure supplies needed for a manufacturer, or handle the clerical duties of a distribution manager. A bachelor's degree makes it possible to start a little further up the ladder in a position like operations research analyst or process associate.

A typical supply chain is composed of many moving parts. Without understanding all the elements, it is difficult to do a good job at any point along the chain. Companies with complex operations have structured training programs for logistics trainees who will learn the operations from the ground up. The trainees will rotate through all the relevant departments, spending enough time in each to grasp the key factors that drive cost and efficiency there.

Career Growth

As logistics workers gain experience, they take on more advanced roles that require analytical and critical thinking. Some of the steps on the career ladder may include industry analyst, project manager, operations director, transportation director, and global logistics manager, to name a few. Logistics management is increasingly involved in international activities, which provide logistics managers a great deal of insight into international business. Those who have successfully developed relationships with foreign partners anywhere within the supply chain and are familiar with international laws, regulations, and customs, are good candidates for interesting positions in international business.

Logistics is a versatile career that offers opportunities to move into specialized areas. For example, disaster response is a field that is highly dependent on efficient logistics. Logistics managers who specialize in this work coordinate the responses to man-made and natural disasters like hurricanes, major wildfires, and oil spills. They make sure the right equipment, supplies, and people for the job arrive quickly and at the right location.

In some cases, a logistics manager might have specialized expertise in a niche area. There are opportunities for them to work as consultants, interacting with a variety of organizations nationally and abroad. This is a good option for those with an entrepreneurial bent to work where and when they want, with clients that interest them.

LOGISTICS PROS TELL THEIR STORIES

I Transitioned From the Army to a Civilian Job

"I was a quartermaster in the Army. My job was to make sure the soldiers in the field had what they needed to complete their mission. Equipment could be big and difficult to move around. Supplies were usually distributed through aerial delivery, often to inhospitable environments. Today, I am a logistics coordinator for a global logistics company. The work is nearly identical, in essence, to what I did in the Army.

My job is to get very large things into difficult places at exactly the right time. My team ships equipment and supplies worldwide to support major construction projects. I personally oversee tracking and monitoring of all cross-border transportation activities. That includes making sure all local and national government regulatory requirements are met. That's important because on the scale we work, violations can result in big fines. I also train new staff and act as liaison to senior management.

The work is much the same, but I now earn a lot more – nearly twice my Army salary, but the money is only icing on the cake. As a veteran, I enjoy working alongside other vets (more than half of my coworkers were in the service). I get to enjoy that same kind of camaraderie I experienced while on active duty. It's also an exciting job. Working on coordinating large-scale logistics strategies with a multinational firm is challenging, and that's the fun. The projects are constantly changing. One day I might need to figure out how to get a monster machine from California to Brazil. The next, I might be shipping building supplies to the next site of the Olympics.

If you're a vet or soon to be one, I encourage you to consider working in logistics. It's a natural career choice if you've had anything to do with transportation, moving people around, ordering supplies and provisions, or planning field exercises. It's all part of logistics, and your experience and leadership skills make you a valuable asset. There is a reason the logistics industry is loaded with vets. There are so many possible roles, from location tech all the way up the ladder. I assure you, there is a place for you."

I Am a Humanitarian Logistics Specialist

"When I was in college, a professor introduced me to the logistics field with his tales of working with Doctors Without Borders. While on sabbatical he had spent a year with that organization, being flown around the world to help organize emergency refugee camps, get vaccines to remote areas, and arrange food supplies. I was enthralled with the stories and changed my major to supply chain management. I have now worked within the humanitarian aid sector for more than 10 years.

My first assignment took me to an extremely

challenging environment in Africa. I quickly learned how difficult and sometimes dangerous getting life-saving supplies to desperately needy people could be. That experience did prepare me for the rigors of logistics in the areas that have been devastated by man-made and natural disasters.

Logistics is usually thought of as a commercial necessity, but it is one of the pillars in relief and disaster management. Humanitarian logistics is a specialized area that is focused on warehousing and distributing supplies during sudden emergencies or natural calamities. It is only the purpose that makes it different from commercial logistics. It utilizes the same skills, like people management, leadership, information gathering, negotiation, and problem solving. Of course there are also functional aspects you need to learn about like transportation, warehousing, sourcing and procurement, customs, and supply chain software.

Working in humanitarian logistics has been very rewarding. I get so much satisfaction from knowing I'm helping to save lives or at least providing relief and hope in the midst of a disaster. I know logistics isn't for everyone, but if problem solving is your thing and you have a passion for helping people in the most dire circumstances, it could be a great career choice. You can find out what it's really like by volunteering for any of the many nonprofit relief organizations."

PERSONAL QUALIFICATIONS

GOOD LOGISTICS MANAGERS TYPICALLY have a good head for math and are very comfortable using business planning software to analyze data and make sound decisions. They might have a degree in math, statistics, or business management, but what sets the successful managers apart is not their education. It is a variety of soft skills that can be taken from one company to another, be applied to any position, and help them ensure things go smoothly no matter what. For example, the number one quality needed for a career in logistics is **good time management skills.** A seemingly small delay of just one hour at one end of a supply chain can create a ripple effect that results in a two-week delay at the other end of the line. If a box of bolts is not delivered on time, it can shut down a whole factory. Here are some other soft skills that are vital to the success of logistics managers.

Critical thinking is crucial. Logistics managers must be able to think on their feet whenever issues arise – which is often. The world of logistics is in a constant state of flux, and it is essential to be able to make quick decisions in order to avoid cost overruns. Good critical thinking skills are needed to analyze the immediate problem, weigh the pros and cons for short and long term fixes, and determine the best solution.

Adaptability is needed in the logistics field where the only thing that is constant is change. The best managers are forward thinkers, able to accurately predict needs and outcomes anywhere in the entire supply chain. They develop contingency plans to prepare for problems that may or may not arise. They must also be able to handle the inevitable, unforeseen issues, such as blizzards, natural disasters, and labor strikes. You will really excel if you are always ready to quickly make last minute adjustments to plans.

Positive people skills are needed every day. The work will bring you into contact with people of all types, from workers to bosses, and suppliers to customers. You never know who you will interact with next. For operations to run smoothly, you need to create instant rapport and develop relationships with everyone along the supply chain. Good managers cultivate those relationships through effective communication. There is no room for miscommunication in the logistics industry. You must be able to clearly state your expectations while actively listening to and acknowledging the input from others.

Teamwork is essential for the success of every aspect of logistics work. Good logistics managers understand that it pays to treat everyone with respect and professionalism. Every word and every action affects other people down the line, and ultimately the outcome of the operation. As a manager, you will use your leadership skills to direct, teach, and motivate your team. Getting your team members to work effectively together sometimes means providing guidance and encouragement to members who are lagging. At all times, you need to lead by example.

Organizational skills are needed to avoid small everyday issues from becoming costly mistakes. The supply chain has numerous tiers and components. Managing them all is a big responsibility. As a logistics manager, you need to devise a system for reviewing and keeping tabs on even the smallest things. Juggling several projects at once in a fast-paced environment with hard deadlines can be stressful. A good logistics manager does not try to handle it all alone. Effective managers organize the tasks at hand and delegate jobs to the most appropriate team members.

ATTRACTIVE FEATURES

LOGISTICS HAS BEEN HIGH ON EVERY PUBLISHED LIST of "best jobs" for years with very good reasons. For starters, the job prospects are good, job satisfaction is high, and earnings are excellent. There are numerous other factors contributing to the high rankings.

Opportunities Abound

Logistics is an expanding field that experiences growth even in recessions. The opportunities seem limitless, with many different roles and work settings. Places of employment vary from big corporations, small business, not-for-profit organizations, and local or federal government entities. You can live almost anywhere and find a good position. Staying close to home is just as viable as moving to a major metro area. If you have bigger dreams, you can even live abroad. Global logistics companies have offices in all the countries they serve.

Low Barrier to Entry

Logistics offers the opportunity to land a high-paying job with only a bachelor's degree, and an individual can get started with even less education than that. The logistics industry values people of all qualification levels, and careers can be launched at any education level, whether it is a high school diploma or a master's degree.

Military veterans also do well in logistics. They often find that four years of service is often enough experience to score a mid-level position, with all the perks that implies, in a civilian organization. In short, if you are good with people and possess the necessary soft skills, companies will want to hire you.

Job Stability

Once you get started, your job is safe. Logistics is not going anywhere and you do not have to either. The US alone spent a whopping $1.5 trillion on logistics in one recent year, according to the annual State of Logistics Report issued by the Supply Chain Management Professionals (CSCMP). Jobs in this field are typically permanent, which means you will have a job until you are ready to retire. There are plenty of opportunities for advancement along the way, too. If you are good at your job, meaning you are able to find ways to solve problems on the fly, you will soar through the ranks.

Good Money

Logistics jobs pay well. In fact, the median base salary for a logistics manager is $100,000 with some earning upwards of $120,000, according to industry reports. Across the board, the median annual pay for individuals in this field is about $75,000.

Travel

Most people only dream of traveling the world. Those working in logistics not only get to travel, they get paid for doing it. The growing world economy has created the need for logistics experts to visit far-flung, often exotic places where companies do business. Although these are business trips that focus far more on work than sightseeing, they open up a whole new world of opportunities in the field of international business. If you have foreign language skills, you will be even more valuable to your employer, and you can pick and choose your destinations.

Fulfilling Work

Although steady employment and high pay are a strong lure to enter this career, most choose to remain because the work is so rewarding. As a logistics manager, many people within the organization's supply chain will rely on you to make sure that everything gets to the right place at the right time. It is your hard work and diligence that makes everyone's job run smoothly, and that can be highly fulfilling.

There is also plenty of room for creativity. Do you love to innovate and think big? If you can come up with new ways to improve transportation, use technology, lower costs, or promote sustainability, there is a logistics company willing to pay you for your ideas.

UNATTRACTIVE ASPECTS

LOGISTICS OFFERS SOLID OPPORTUNITIES for career progression, but working your way up will have its challenges. The work can be stressful because it is fast-paced and there is no room for error. Mistakes can be very costly to the company you work for. When the unexpected occurs, you will have to deal with unhappy people who depend on you to keep things rolling smoothly so they can do their jobs. In this high-pressured environment, you need to stay calm and work quickly to solve any problems that arise. On the plus side, those who maneuver through the sticky situations often earn promotions into less stressful positions.

Career advancement is one of the core attractions of this career, however, it usually requires more education. Without it, it can be a dead end job. After mastering the basics, managers typically want to move up to managing a department. At minimum, getting into that position would require a Project Management Professional (PMP) certification. That takes 35 to 50 education hours to earn, depending on where you get it. The alternative is to obtain a master's degree in Operations Research/Industrial Engineering (OR/IE), or maybe an MBA (Master of Business Administration degree). This is a serious commitment to the field, but going back to school will pay off. In fact, promotions are typically forthcoming within a few months.

The work locations in this field are varied. In many cases, work locations are mobile, requiring travel part of the time or even 100 percent of the time. There may be an office somewhere with your name on the door, but you may rarely see it. This could seem exciting at first, but it can grow tiresome, especially if you want to have a stable family life. Companies expect a high level of commitment, so it is essential to ask about the work environment and understand what will be expected of you before accepting a position.

Logistics is a crucial link in the supply chain sphere so there is little, if any, flexibility when it comes to working hours or job sharing. Almost no one in this field works fewer than 40 hours a week, and many put in more than that. In some cases, you can create your own schedule as long as you get the job done. You still have to put in the hours, even if that means working 40 hours in three days.

EDUCATION AND TRAINING

ASPIRING LOGISTICS MANAGERS HAVE SEVERAL options to consider when preparing for this career. Which path you choose will depend on your career goals, availability of relevant training, and how fast you want to get started. A position as a logistics manager typically requires a bachelor's degree, although an associate degree may suffice. In some cases, related work experience may substitute for education – especially if that experience was obtained in the military. There are also certificate programs offered by vocational-tech schools that are good for landing entry- level positions. There are also internships and internal training programs, usually referred to as apprenticeships. Beginners should consider these options carefully before choosing which direction to take.

Internships and Apprenticeships

Logistics dedicated training programs are offered by employers and third party firms that specialize in this kind of training. The programs can last anywhere from 12 weeks to two years. Typically, the first 12 to 16 weeks involves classroom instruction two or three days a week. The other days are spent getting on-the-job training under the supervision of an assigned mentor. The trainee will rotate through the various departments to gain a well-rounded understanding of the company's supply chain operations. Once the program is completed successfully, the trainee may be offered a permanent position, but still under the direct supervision of a mentor. This usually means starting in a lower position such as receiving manager or configuration analyst, with the understanding that there will be a transition into a logistics management position when the company is satisfied that the trainee has demonstrated proficiency. The programs are designed to be rigorous, and some companies have an expected dropout rate and do not guarantee placement at the end of training.

Substituting Work Experience

It is not uncommon for employers to accept work experience in place of a specific degree. However, the work experience must be directly related to logistics, supply chains, or business operations. The most likely candidates are those who have been assigned to a logistical support role in the military, such as warehouse supervisor or transportation coordinator. Logistics is very important to the military and your service usually provides enough experience for a mid-level position in logistics management. Former service members also bring leadership skills to the table, something that employers actively look for in candidates.

Tech Certificate

Many candidates obtain a position in logistics by completing a vocational logistics program offered by a community or traditional college or a technical school. These certificate programs typically offer one-year programs that include courses in production control, purchasing and materials control, inventory control strategies, and transportation management. It may be difficult to find these programs in some areas, but there are now many schools that offer online logistics programs at all education levels.

Bachelor's Degree

A growing number of employers prefer candidates with a bachelor's degree due to the increased complexity of the field. A degree is also necessary to advance in a wider range of jobs today. College majors should be in systems engineering, supply chain management, or a business-related field with courses in finance, logistics, and IT. Most programs train students on software and technologies commonly used in logistics, such as radio-frequency identification (RFID).

Some schools offer a degree in transportation and logistics, which focuses on transporting large volumes of waste or chemicals. In these programs, students learn to transport hazardous materials and to dispose of them in the most effective and safe way. Typical courses cover hazardous material transportation, logistics and management operations, international logistics management, and air transportation. This is a growing field of specialization that is rapidly expanding globally.

Master's Degree

Logistics managers aiming for top leadership roles often obtain a master's degree in supply chain management, industrial engineering, business, or finance. Master's degree programs focus on skills such as management, accounting and systems dynamics, global logistics, sustainable supply chains, and other industry-specific applications. Students are generally allowed to hone in on certain areas of interest and specialization.

Regardless of the education level going in, ongoing education will be necessary throughout your career. Software is constantly changing, entire fields are being disrupted, and world markets are constantly evolving.

Certifications

You do not need to be licensed or certified to become a logistics manager, but professional certification can demonstrate competence and knowledge needed for higher-level jobs. Certification is available from several professional organizations, such as the International Society of Logistics, American Society of Transportation and Logistics, or APICS. To obtain certification, the candidate must meet certain education and work experience requirements and pass an exam.

EARNINGS

THE AVERAGE ANNUAL BASE SALARY for a logistics manager in the US is about $100,000. The lowest 10 percent earn less than $50,000, and the highest 10 percent earn more than $125,000. That is a fairly wide salary range. How much any individual in this career might expect to make depends on several factors, including the type of industry, geographic location, skill sets, and experience level.

It is also common for logistics managers to receive additional cash compensation, which significantly boosts total income. This may include bonuses, commissions, tips, and profit sharing. The additional compensation averages $7,500, but ranges from $2,500 to $20,000, depending mostly on job level and employer policies.

The highest paying jobs for logistics managers are in the federal government, where salaries run about 10 percent higher than average. The lowest are in the wholesale trade and third party logistics services, which pay about 10 percent lower than average. This is not surprising since these are basically intermediaries that have to carve out enough to make a profit while promising to save clients money. Some of the better paying employers are retailers that are big enough to handle their own logistics. Big box stores like Home Depot and mammoth retailers like Walmart have entire facilities staffed with logistics managers who are paid better than average salaries.

There is a positive trend toward greater pay for logistics managers who gain experience over a period of years. Entry-level pay usually starts out averaging $50,000. That steadily grows and eventually doubles by mid-career.

Location heavily influences pay rates. The highest paying jobs are in San Francisco (where pay is 40 percent higher than the national average), Seattle, and Boston. These are important seaports where logistics managers with global trade experience are in high demand. Being a seaport is not the primary reason for the higher pay, however. In fact, other port cities like Los Angeles, San Diego, and New York pay below average salaries. The difference is that some port cities are tech hubs and others are not. San Francisco, of course, is part of the Silicon Valley, Seattle is where international cargo vessels come and go between Asia and tech giants like Microsoft, and Boston is a global tech startup incubator.

The lowest paying locations are mostly in the south. For example, employers in Charlotte, Louisville, and Austin pay logistics managers about 10 percent less than the national average. It is important to note the difference in cost of living between high-paying and low-paying cities, which can effectively level the playing field.

There are many different skills that can be applied to this work. Some are more valuable than others. Logistics managers who are skilled in budget management, contract negotiations, inventory management, and leadership receive pay boosts which can amount to seven to nine percent above average. On the other hand, skills like customer service, which are often highly touted as essential, have no effect at all on pay.

Education by itself does not significantly impact salaries at the start of a career. Consider someone with a high school diploma or tech certificate who gets a foot in the door of a logistics company through an internship. That individual's salary would be roughly the same as someone starting out with a bachelor's degree. However, without a college degree, advancement will be elusive. To get promoted into desirable positions requires at least a bachelor's degree. A master's degree will be needed to make it to the top of the career ladder where salaries average between $125,000 and $150,000.

The vast majority of logistics managers work full time, and nearly one in four works more than 40 hours a week. Although additional hours are commonly needed to ensure that operations stay on schedule, most logistics managers are salaried and therefore do not generally receive overtime pay.

OPPORTUNITIES

LOGISTICS IS A BIG BUSINESS. According to an annual report from the Council of Supply Chain Management Professionals (CSCMP), the US alone currently spends a whopping $1.5 trillion a year on logistics. Good logistical management is essential to a company's profitability. Supply and distribution systems are becoming more complex, which makes it even more challenging to gain an edge. This has created opportunities across the industry for talented and well-trained professionals who can figure out how to move products more efficiently at minimal cost. About 150,000 people are working in this career now. It is estimated that 10,000 more will be needed within 10 years. Job opportunities abound in almost every sector, from retail to finance to government.

To appreciate the enormity of the opportunities, one should look beyond our borders. This is a growing field that is set to expand globally. Skilled logistics managers are in high demand as companies of all sizes compete for top positions in the global marketplace. Global logistics spending is expected to exceed $10.5 trillion in just a few years, according to a new report. Qualified individuals who want to experience life in another culture will find ample opportunities to do so, living and working abroad. Those who are fluent in a foreign language are particularly valued.

As transportation costs continue to rise, there is a sense of extreme urgency and pressure to deliver on time and under budget. Technology is expected to play an increasingly vital role in meeting the challenge of global logistics. Supply chain digitization – the process of using the latest tech solutions to redesign logistics practices – is widely viewed as the future of this fast-paced, highly competitive environment. Therefore, prospects are best for candidates who are very comfortable using advanced computer software and hardware. This is perfect for veterans who have done logistical work for the military. A recent degree in logistics management from a program that prominently features coursework in emerging software platforms and other relevant technologies is also welcome.

This career field is hidden behind the scenes. While highly visible fields like finance and healthcare attract many aspiring professionals, logistics is often overlooked. Recruiters and employers find it difficult to fill vital positions because people with the right set of soft and hard skills rarely give it the consideration it deserves. This has created a shortage of interested candidates, which is good news for those who do appreciate the rewards this career can offer. When a career flies under the radar there is less competition, and those with even modest credentials will most likely land a job. It is unclear how long this window of opportunity will remain open though. It is fast becoming an area of interest for a new generation of college graduates. According to a report from the Association for Supply Chain Management, there is a growing number of millennials who see logistics management as a ripe opportunity for career growth.

There are also many paths for career advancement. With the right combination of education, experience, and performance, a logistics manager can achieve a department head position and even executive roles such as Chief Operating Officer (COO) or Vice President of Operations.

GETTING STARTED

EVEN THOUGH THERE ARE THOUSANDS of job openings in the growing field of logistics, finding a job will require preparation on your part. When you search online for "logistics" jobs, you will notice there are many different job titles and few of them simply say "logistics." The good news is there are multiple options. You will have to narrow your search to find the right one for you.

There are several ways to identify what kind of job you would like to start with (and rule out the jobs you do not want). The first is job shadowing several positions at a local logistics company. Getting some experience first-hand will put you ahead during interviews. Next, look for internships and apprenticeships. These are offered by many logistic companies, usually during the summer. In addition to being able to sample the various positions, these can be stepping stones to entry-level employment. In fact, it is common for companies that offer paid internships to make permanent job offers to interns upon program completion. You can also learn about the industry by attending trade shows or reaching out to companies that interest you. This is an "invisible" industry that not many people know about so those within the industry are more than happy to talk to anyone who is interested about their experiences and challenges.

Now that you know where you might fit in the logistic industry, it is time to create a good résumé. You can get help from your school's career office. There are also numerous websites that provide free résumé writing help, advice, and samples. You might not have an impressive résumé yet, but you can stand out if you include some logistics industry lingo or keywords.

Ambitious job seekers create their own website or blog that acts as an online portfolio. It could include a printable PDF of your résumé and cover letter, letters of recommendation, etc. At the very least, you should create an online profile on sites like LinkedIn. It is an accepted tool employers and recruiters use to find new employees. Just make sure your profile is professional. You want to be searchable in a good way, and you can search for and apply for jobs there, too.

Start your real job search online. There are many different job search websites out there. You can find an abundance of logistics jobs on the big ones like Indeed, ZipRecruiter, Glassdoor, and LinkedIn. There are also websites that are dedicated to the logistics industry like JobsinLogistics.com and IHireLogistics.com.

Many jobs are never advertised. The only way to find them is to connect to employers through networking. If you attended a school with a career office, contact them to ask for advice and connections to alumni. If you are in an internship or apprenticeship, ask your supervisor about job openings. You can also ask coworkers to introduce you to others in the field or at specific companies you would like to work for. It is also a good idea to attend conferences and professional gatherings. These events are often posted on sites like LinkedIn or in national publications. Make sure to bring copies of your résumé and do not be shy about letting people know you are ready to start your career in logistics.

ASSOCIATIONS

- **Association for Supply Chain Management (ASCM)**
https://www.ascm.org

- **International Society of Logistics (SOLE)**
http://www.sole.org

- **American Society of Transportation and Logistics (APICS)**
http://www.apics.org

- **Council of Supply Chain Management Professionals (CSCMP)**
https://cscmp.org

- **Warehousing Education and Research Council**
https://werc.org

PERIODICALS

- **3PL Wire: Third Party Logistics News**
http://www.3plwire.com

- **Journal of Commerce: Logistics Newsletter**
https://www.joc.com

- **Logistics Quarterly**
http://www.logisticsquarterly.com

- **Logistics Management**
https://www.logisticsmgmt.com

WEBSITES

- **JobsinLogistics.com**
https://www.jobsinlogistics.com

- **IhireLogistics.com**
https://www.ihirelogistics.com

Copyright 2019
Institute For Career Research

CAREERS INTERNET DATABASE
www.careers-internet.org

www.ingramcontent.com/pod-product-compliance
Lightning Source LLC
Chambersburg PA
CBHW051206170526
45158CB00005B/1843